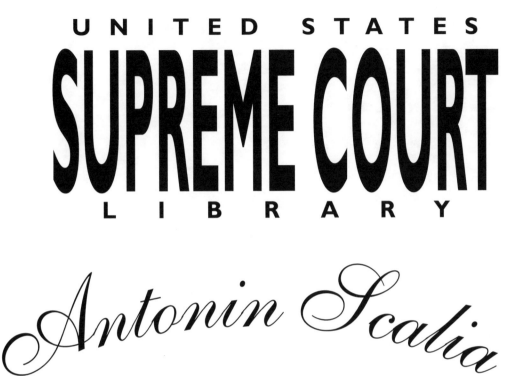

UNITED STATES
SUPREME COURT
LIBRARY

Antonin Scalia

by Bob Italia

Published by Abdo & Daughters, 6535 Cecilia Circle, Edina, Minnesota 55439.

Copyright © 1992 by Abdo Consulting Group, Inc., Pentagon Tower, P.O. Box 36036, Minneapolis, Minnesota 55435. International copyrights reserved in all counties. No part of this book may be reproduced in any form without written permission from the publisher. Printed in the United States.

Photo credits: A/P Wide World Photos-cover, 4, 7, 8, 22, 27, 31
                   Archive Photos-10, 13, 34
                   FPG International-18
                   UPI/Bettmann-6, 15, 21, 24, 32, 37

Edited by: Paul Deegan

Library of Congress Cataloging-in-Publication Data

Italia, Robert, 1955-
      Antonin Scalia / written by Bob Italia ; [edited by Paul Deegan].
         p. cm. — (Supreme Court justices)
      Includes index.
      Summary: A career biography of Supreme Court Associate Justice Antonin Scalia.
      ISBN 1-56239-093-7
      1. Scalia, Antonin—Juvenile literature. 2. Judges—United States—Biography—Juvenile
literature. [1. Scalia, Antonin. 2. Judges. 3. United States. Supreme Court—Biography.] I.
Deegan, Paul J., 1937- . II. Title. III. Series.
      KF8745.S33I83 1992
      347.73'2634—dc20
      [B]
      [347.3073534]
      [B]
                                                                      92-13712
                                                                      CIP
Second Printing, 1994   AC

Table of Contents

Page

5   A Defender of the American Dream

6   The Son of an Immigrant

11 The Beginning of a Law Career

14 Antonin Scalia Goes to Washington

17 Out of Work and On the Move

19 Scalia Breezes to the Supreme Court

26 Is He Conservative or Liberal?

33 Antonin Scalia Up Close

38 A Defender of Constitutional Rights

39 Glossary

40 Index

A Defender of the American Dream

United States Supreme Court Associate Justice Antonin Scalia has become an inspiration to hard-working Americans everywhere. He rose from humble beginnings to the peak of the legal profession. He showed that the American dream is still alive and well if a person can overcome obstacles through dedication and hard work.

Despite being labeled a conservative, Antonin Scalia remains his own man. Through his many Supreme Court opinions,

Antonin Scalia poses with his family in his chambers, 1986.

Scalia has shown a keen legal mind and superior intelligence while staunchly defending our Constitutional rights— even when it meant drawing criticism from conservative and liberals alike.

The Son of an Immigrant

Antonin Scalia was born March 11, 1936 in Trenton, New Jersey. He was named after his grandfather, Antonio, a mechanic in Sicily. Scalia was called "Nino" by his family and friends.

Scalia's father, Eugene, came to America as a teenager. He worked various jobs while studying hard at school, and married the daughter of another Italian immigrant. Eventually, Eugene Scalia became a professor of Romance languages (French, Italian, Spanish) at Brooklyn College in New York.

Scalia attended Xavier High School, a well-known Catholic school in New York City, where he graduated first in his class. Classmates recalled that Scalia already had developed conservative political views—views that he would carry throughout his life.

Scalia as Macbeth in his high school play.

Scalia first came to Washington, D.C. to attend Georgetown University. There he again proved to be a brilliant student. During his junior year, Scalia studied abroad at the University of Fribourg in Switzerland. Returning to Georgetown, he received his bachelor's degree in 1957, graduating first in his class.

Scalia's graduation picture from the Xavier High School yearbook.

The Beginning of a Law Career

Scalia went on to study law at Harvard Law School in Cambridge, Massachusetts. There he became the note editor of the Harvard Law Review.

Scalia graduated magna cum laude from Havard in 1960. Afterward, Scalia married Maureen McCarthy, who had just graduated from Radcliffe College.

Brooklyn College, New York, where Eugene Scalia was a professor of romance languages.

Scalia and his wife moved to Cleveland, Ohio where Scalia joined the law firm of Jones, Day, Cockley and Reavis. At a party given for the new-comers of the law firm, Scalia dazzled his elder colleagues with discussions of current legal questions. All were impressed with Scalia's energy and intellect.

Scalia gained much legal experience in Cleveland, working on a variety of cases. In 1967, Scalia moved his family to Charlottesville, Virginia. There he joined the law faculty of the University of Virginia. Scalia taught until 1971. Then he and his family moved to Washington, D.C, marking Scalia's first big step into politics.

The University of Virginia in Charlottesville. Antonin Scalia was on the faculty from 1967 to 1971.

Antonin Scalia Goes to Washington

Scalia took the general counsel job in the Telecommunications Policy office in the Executive Office of President Richard M. Nixon. A year later, Scalia was named chairman of the Administrative Conference of the United States. This independent government agency studies federal administrative and legal procedures. Then it makes improvement recommendations.

President Richard Nixon.

The Adminstrative Conference is made up of agency heads, departmental officials, and univeristy professors. They know how the government administration works. The experience, knowledge and personal contacts Scalia made at the Conference would be invaluable to him later in life.

14

In 1974, Scalia returned to a government position. President Gerald Ford named him an Assistant Attorney General in the Office of Legal Counsel for the Department of Justice. The Office of Legal Counsel gives legal advice to the president—particularly constitutional issues. Supreme Court Chief Justice William Rehnquist once held the position. During his stay at the Justice Department, Scalia had the opportunity to present a case before the Supreme Court.

Out of Work and On the Move

Scalia was on the move again in the winter of 1977. Democrat Jimmy Carter had won the November 1976 presidential election and appointed his own people to the Justice Department. Republicans like Scalia had to find new jobs.

Scalia worked as a Scholar in Residence at the American Enterprise Institute, a conservative "think-tank" that formed government and business ideas. Scalia also was a visiting professor at Georgetown Law School.

By the fall of 1977, Scalia and his family were in Chicago, Illinois. Scalia had accepted a teaching position at the University of Chicago Law School. In 1981 Scalia spent a year teaching at Stanford University in California.

Scalia Breezes to the Supreme Court

Scalia returned to the political scene in Washington, D. C. on July 15, 1982. President Ronald Reagan nominated Scalia to be a judge on the U.S. Court of Appeals. Scalia had no problems being confirmed. He took his oath of office in August.

In 1986, William Rehnquist was elevated from Associate Justice to Chief Justice. This move created a vacancy on the Supreme Court. President Reagan nominated Antonin Scalia to the position. Then Scalia, according to the Constitution, had to be approved by the United States Senate.

When he was elected president, Democrat Jimmy Carter appointed his own people to the Justice Department. Republicans like Scalia had to find new jobs.

Senator Strom Thurmond was the Chairman of the Senate Judiciary Committee. This committee was in charge of evaluating Supreme Court Justice candidates. Thurmond opened Scalia's confirmation hearing by describing the qualities needed by a Supreme Court Justice.

Said Senator Thurmond: "A Supreme Court Justice needs integrity, courage, knowledge of the law, compassion, judicial temperment, and an understanding of and appreciation for the majesty of our system of government."

President Reagan (r) nominated Scalia to Associate Justice of the Supreme Court in 1986.

Thurmond then added that he believed Antonin Scalia had always possessed those qualities. The rest of the Judiciary Committee echoed Senator Thurmond's high regard for Scalia.

Scalia breezed through the confirmation process. The Senate Judiciary Committee voted unanimously to recommend Antonin Scalia's nomination as Associate Justice. When the rest of the Senate voted, the approval was unanimous.

Scalia's confirmation was in stark contrast to the ordeal William Rehnquist had to endure before being voted Chief Justice. Rehnquist received 33 negative votes from the Senate. No previous nominee had ever received so many no votes before being approved.

Scalia (l) and Rehnquist shake hands outside the Supreme Court building in Washington, D.C., 1986.

Scalia's appointment to the Supreme Court was cheered by the Italian-American community. They believed that the appointment contained an important message. No matter who you are or where you come from, you can become anything you want if you work hard for it. Considering the Scalia family's humble beginnings, the American dream was indeed still alive.

Scalia is sworn in as Associate Justice of the Supreme Court by Chief Justice Warren Burger September 26,1986.

Is He Conservative or Liberal?

Many people wondered what kind of justice Antonin Scalia would turn out to be. Would he remain conservative, or would he turn out to be someone very different?

Scalia's record supports both views. Scalia takes liberal views when considering issues of free speech. But when it comes to issues such as affirmative action and property rights, Scalia usually votes conservatively.

Scalia also has surprised many with his consistent defense of criminal rights. But Scalia insists that he is not

Scalia's words draw criticism from conservatives around the country.

necessarily defending the rights of criminals but rights granted by the Constitution.

One of his first cases involved the use of a one-way screen to hide a victim from the defendant during a trial. Scalia wrote that the use of the screen violated the defendant's right to see who had brought charges against him.

"Face-to-face presence may, unfortunately, upset the truthful victim or abused child," Scalia wrote. "But by the same token it may confound and undo the false accuser, or reveal the child coached by a malevolent adult. It is a truism that constitutional protections have costs."

Scalia was concerned that the screen would make it easier for a false accuser to lie because the accuser would not have to see the defendant face-to-face. It is much harder to lie about someone if we have to look directly at them.

Most Supreme Court Justices agreed with Scalia's opinion. They overruled the conviction against the defendant. Those who disagreed with Scalia included Chief Justice William Rehnquist.

Scalia's words drew much criticism from many conservatives around the country. They could not believe that a fellow conservative could state an unsympathetic opinion against the police and the victim of crime. But Scalia defended his opinion. He was protecting the Constitutional right of the defendant, he said.

In another decision unpopular with conservatives, Scalia sided with the majority of his colleagues in a flag burning case. The majority decided that individual states could not make it a crime to burn the American flag. Scalia again pointed out that the First Amendment of the Constitution grants Americans the right of freedom of expression, no matter how unpopular that expression may be.

Scalia suprised many in yet another case. The case concerned the drug testing of railroad employees involved in train accidents. Scalia voted in favor of the tests.

The defendants claimed the drug testing violated their Constitutional rights. But Scalia believed that if drugs used by railroad workers could cause harm to others, then drug testing should be allowed.

Justice Scalia was expected to be a staunch defender of the rights of individual states. That assumption turned out to be false.

Official Supreme Court portrait, 1990.

Scalia often has voted in favor of the federal government's intervention on state and local matters. One case involved a state's right to set a legal drinking age. Scalia agreed with the majority of justices that the federal government could force individual states to raise the legal drinking age to 21 if those states received federal highway funds.

This does not mean that Scalia always favors increasing the federal government's influence and power over individual states. Scalia has consistently voted for tax reductions and reducing government regulations.

Antonin Scalia Up Close

Justice Scalia is a hard-working man. He often reviews a case the night before it is presented before the Supreme Court. And he writes his opinions for each case on a word processor at his desk.

Scalia does not rely on his clerks to summarize the key issues of each case, as most justices do. His four law clerks assist him in the decision-making process by researching cases and through open discussions.

Scalia persistently questions attorneys during cases, looking for inconsistancies and lack of evidence.

Scalia is known to persistently question attorneys during a case. He usually asks more questions than any of his fellow justices. If the attorney's arguments are inconsistent or lack evidence, Justice Scalia will point out flaws in their arguments.

Justice Scalia has also been known to use the same harsh style on his fellow justices. Instead of simply disagreeing with them, he will attack their way of thinking. Scalia's advice to all who approach him is simple: be prepared to answer questions instead of giving speeches—and know what you're talking about.

Associate Justice Antonin Scalia remains loyal to the defense of our constitutional rights.

At times, Scalia can be impatient. But he is also charming and can be tolerant of those who disagree with him. Scalia also possesses a wry sense of humor.

Not much is known about Antonin Scalia's personal life. He and his wife have raised nine children. The Scalia's now live in a quiet but surprisingly modest neighborhood near the home of Associate Justice Byron White. Scalia and White were friends before Scalia was named to the Supreme Court. Scalia is also a neighbor of Associate Justice Anthony Kennedy, with whom he jogs.

The Scalia's are devout Catholics.
Keeping with family tradition, Scalia named
his first son after his grandfather, Eugene.
Scalia and his wife have raised their
children with the same devotion given
to them by their parents. The Scalia
children have learned the importance and
value of hard work and discipline. After
all, that's something Justice Antonin Scalia,
the only son of an Italian immigrant,
knows very well.

**Antonin Scalia
believes in the
value of hard work
and discipline.**

A Defender of Constitutional Rights

Antonin Scalia's intellect and likeable personal qualities make him an effective and influential spokesman for our Constitutional rights. Many wondered if he would simply vote conservatively. But Justice Scalia remains loyal to the defense of our Constitutional rights—a policy that bodes well for all of America.

Glossary

Conservative: Inclined to keep things as they are or were in the past.

Constitution: The fundamental law of a state which guides and limits the use of power by the government.

Defendant: A person charged with a crime.

Democrat: A member of one of the two main political parties in the United States.

Justice: The determination of rights according to the rules of law.

Liberal: A person favorable to progress or reform.

Republicans: A member of one of the two main political parties in the United States.

Senate: A governing or lawmaking assembly. The Congress of the United States is the Senate and the House of Representatives.

Think-tank: A group organized for interdisciplinary research as in technological and social problems.

Index

Associate Justice-5,19,23,35
Carter, Jimmy-17
Chief Justice-16,19,23,28
Conservative-5,6,17,26,29,38
Constitution-5,19,26,29,30,38
Defendant-28-30
Democrat-17
Ford, Gerald-16
Harvard Law School-11
Immigrant-6,36
Justice Department-16-17
Liberal-5,26
Nixon, Richard-14
Reagan, Ronald-19
Republican-17
Senate Judiciary Committee-20,23
Senater-19-20,23
Stanford University-17
Supreme Court-5,16,19,20,26,28,33,35
United States Court of Appeals-19
University of Chicago-17
University of Virginia-12

PREFACE TO THE SECOND EDITION

Since publishing, in 1963, the first textbook on Project Planning and Control, "FUNDAMENTALS OF PROJECT PLANNING AND CONTROL" (Library of Congress Catalog Card No. 63-13195), the author has accumulated additional insight into, and practical information on the application of the technique of Network Planning (the most common generic name for planning projects by the CRITICAL PATH METHOD (CPM) and PERT (Program Evaluation and Review Technique) to a variety of projects as a practicing consultant in this field. This edition is an expansion of the first basic textbook, with the incorporation of new concepts (Invoiceless Cost Control and the Continuous Milestone Chart); observations (Current Abuses of the Technique, the Negative Float/Slack Fallacy, the limitations of Precedence Diagramming) and re-evaluations (The Time Scale Chart recommendations).

This book is an attempt to present to the line manager the fundamental methodology of a scientific information system. The advanced mathematical concepts of parametric linear programming are left to others. A bibliography is included for those who would be interested in the formal construction and derivation of the technique.

The updating of the material herein is the result of consulting work on over 150 projects of various types and magnitudes, ranging from a small local political campaign effort to the engineering and construction of a $200 million dollar nuclear power plant. Appearance as an expert witness in several arbitration and litigation cases accounts for the thoughts on the use of the technique in litigation and claims. Finally, the author subscribes fully to the Aristotlian theory that, "The Teacher learns more than the Pupil"; the fielding of questions from practical minded engineers and executives in over 100 seminars has forced him to defend, re-evaluate and clarify all aspects of the material herein, from the rudiments to the advanced concepts of multi-project scheduling.

The essence of any business "control" system is the timely, accurate and explicit flow of information. "Control" is a decision-making process, made by humans or groups of humans in concert. The process is contingent on judgements made from available information. The computing machine serves only as a tool to expedite information flow, and its basic manipulations. The methodology unfolded herein is primarily a manual one; allowing the manager to use it on projects of reasonable size. Information is included to determine size, time and cost boundaries, beyond which use of Electronic Data Processing equipment is recommended.

The style of presentation is informal. By making the material more readable, and less pedantic, it was felt that the reader would gain more confidence and understanding in a technique that is really relatively simple.

A. James Waldron
Haddonfield, N. J.
December, 1968

TABLE OF CONTENTS

CHAPTER	TITLE	PAGE
1	Introduction	1
2	Fundamentals of Planning	8
3	Event Numbering	27
4	Collecting Time Estimates	43
5	Establishing The Plan's Time Boundaries	46
6	The Critical Path	56
7	Slack or Float	63
8	Network Schedules (Activity Times)	68
9	Inserting a Target Date	82
10	Program Evaluation and Review Technique (PERT)	87
11A	The Time Scale Chart and Project Control	101
11B	Manpower Allocation	117
	Review	134
	Alternate Strategies	134
	The Decision Tree	139
12	An "Ideal" Project Schedule	143
13	Optimum Schedules Based On Time And Cost	159
14	The Least Total Cost Schedule For A Project	179
15	Installation of Network Systems	218
16	Computer Orientation	225
17	Control of Simultaneous Projects	237
18	Project Reporting and Updating	245
	Updating a Critical Path Schedule	251
	Negative Float or Slack - The Fallacy	262

CHAPTER	TITLE	PAGE
19	Cost Control	278
	The Percent Complete Fallacy	287
	PERT COST	291
	Invoiceless Cost Control	305
20	Precedence Diagramming	310
21	The Continuous Milestone Chart	316
22	The Use of Network Techniques in Claims, Litigations	331
23	Current Abuses Of The Network Technique	361
24	Value Engineering and Network Planning	367
25	Miscellaneous	369
	Appendix	378
	Bibliography	385